D0874319

FRANCE GAGNON PRATTE

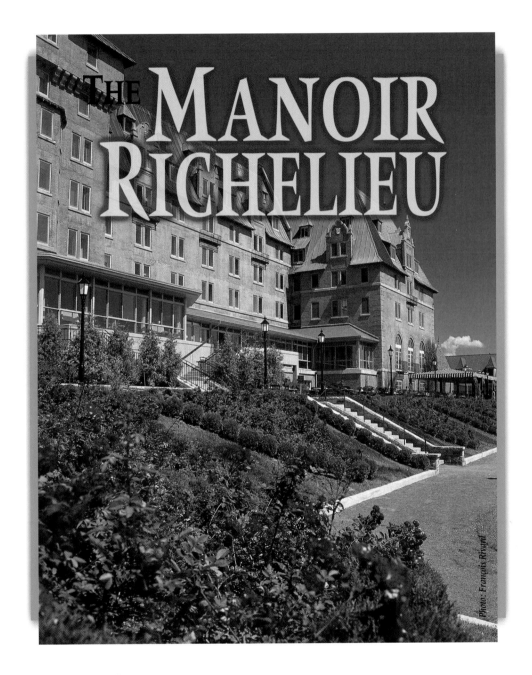

THE MANOIR RICHELIEU

Photo: François Rivard

Fairmont
THE MANOIR RICHELIEU
QUEBEC

ÉDITIONS
CONTINUITÉ

**Canadian Cataloguing in Publication Data**

Gagnon Pratte, France

The Manoir Richelieu

(The great hotels of Canada collection)

Issued also in French under title: Le Manoir Richelieu.

Includes bibliographical references.

ISBN 2-922527-07-7

1. Manoir Richelieu (Pointe-au-Pic, Quebec) - History. 2. Hotels - Quebec (Province) - Pointe-au-Pic - History. 3. Tourism - Quebec (Province) - Charlevoix Region - History. I. Title. II. Collection

TX941.M36G3313 2000          647.94714'49          C00-941609-9

AUTHOR:            France Gagnon Pratte

TRANSLATOR:        Linda Blythe

BOOK DESIGN:       Norman Dupuis inc.

COVER PHOTO:       François Rivard

ELECTRONIC PRE-PRESS:   Compelec inc.

PRINTER:           Imprimerie La Renaissance inc.

Legal deposit - National Library of Québec, 2000

Legal deposit - National Library of Ottawa, 2000

ISBN 2-922527-07-7 (pbk.)

ISBN 2-922527-06-9 (French pbk.)

*This book is dedicated*

*to my granddaughter*

*Béatrix Caroline,*

*a young adventurer*

*who already appreciates*

*the luxurious life*

*of great hotels.*

# TABLE OF CONTENTS

| | | |
|---|---|---|
| *INTRODUCTION* | **The *Malle Baye*** | x |
| | Mount Murray and Murray Bay | 3 |
| **PART 1** | **The Manoir Richelieu** | 9 |
| | The Richelieu & Ontario Navigation Company | 9 |
| | The First Hotel: A Palatial Wooden Structure overlooking the St. Lawrence River | 11 |
| | The Manoir Richelieu Golf Club | 17 |
| **PART 2** | **The Second Manoir** | 23 |
| | John S. Archibald | 23 |
| | A Château on High | 30 |
| | The Good Life | 38 |
| | Fishing in Charlevoix | 52 |
| | Snowy Weather | 54 |
| **PART 3** | **Hard Times** | 63 |
| **PART 4** | **Sleeping Beauty Awakes** | 67 |
| | The Height of Refined Elegance | 70 |
| | A Casino for Charlevoix | 78 |
| | Centennial Celebration | 82 |
| *CONCLUSION:* | **Rebirth of a Legend** | 83 |
| | BIBLIOGRAPHY | 85 |
| | ACKNOWLEDGEMENTS | 86 |

Like the legendary phoenix, the Manoir Richelieu is born again... Beginning its second hundred years, faithful to its glorious past, the hotel once more opens its doors to heads of state, the greats of this world, poets and lovers alike. This is truly a cause for celebration.

[translation]

**Philippe Borel**
*Regional Vice-President and*
*General Manager of the Château Frontenac*

For over a century, the enchantingly beautiful Manoir Richelieu was a haven for Canadian and American summer visitors who appreciated its romantic and exclusive nature. Now, the Manoir has recovered its atmosphere of days gone by and a legend has been reborn.

[translation]

**Alex Kassatly**
*General Manager*
*The Manoir Richelieu*

# THE MALLE BAYE

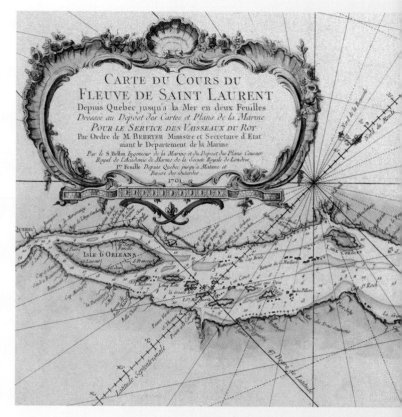

It was Samuel de Champlain who coined the name Malle Baye when he passed through in 1608 on his way to Québec after stopping at Tadoussac. In his diary, *Les voyages de la Nouvelle-France occidentale, dicte Canada,* Champlain described it like this:

> *From there, we reached another cape we named Cap à l'Aigle, distant 8 leagues from Cap Dauphin. Between the two lies a large cove, at the bottom of which is a little stream which dries up at low tide; we called it "the flat river," or* malle baye.

Champlain could not have given a more appropriate name to this inhospitable harbour where he was unable to anchor. Forty years would go by before any more interest was shown in the place: in 1653, the governor of New France, Jean de Lauzon, granted land there to surveyor-general Jean Bourdon so that he could start a small settlement. The estate extended from Cap-aux-Oies to below Malbaie River. Jean Bourdon, who was kept very busy by his responsibilities as the king's procurator-general, neglected his role as a colonist and eventually abandoned the estate. Then, on November 7, 1672, Administrator Talon granted the seigneury to Philippe Gaultier de Comporté, making him the first seigneur (or feudal lord) of La Malbaye. A half century later, after passing through several different hands, the seigneury was sold to the king of France for twenty thousand shillings. In 1895, the *Bulletin des recherches historiques* describes the land returned by deed of sale to the crown as follows:

> [translation]
>
> *The land, fief and seigneury of La Malbaye, consisting roughly of about six leagues of frontage by four in depth, meeting on one side to the west the lands of the King's farmers, commonly referred to as the Tadoussac farms, and along with the sawmills and flour mills…*
>
> (Roy, 1895).

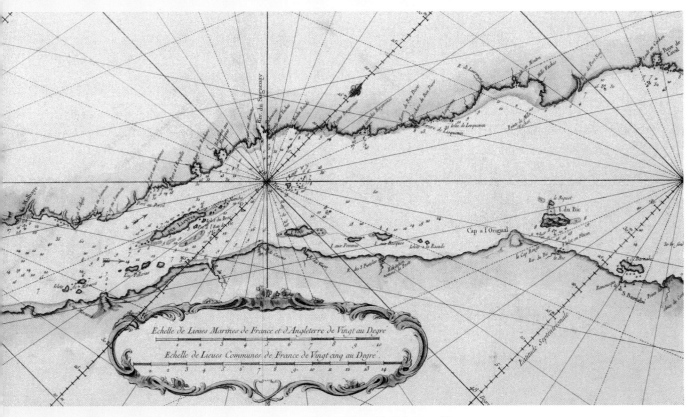

*Part of a chart of the St. Lawrence River by Nicolas Bellin, 1761.*
*ANQ, EC no. 22*

Under French rule, the seigneury of La Malbaie was essentially a huge farm, and not important enough to justify developing the area. It represented a failure of New France's colonization policy.

It was not until the end of the war with the British Empire and the French defeat, in 1759, that the region finally began to grow, thanks to a number of British and Scottish newcomers who were to breath new life into the devastated colony.

Philippe Gaultier de Comporté
at Malbaie, New France, 1672,
*a watercolour by Charles W. Jefferys,*
*1929 PAC, C-40597*

# Mount Murray and Murray Bay

When the British regiments were demobilized after the conquest, the king of England authorized the governors to grant land to officers and soldiers in order to populate the conquered land and to keep a military elite in place that would be prepared to take up arms if need be.

Thus, on April 27, 1762, General Murray granted the huge seigneury of La Malbaie to two distinguished officers of the Seventy-eighth Fraser Highlanders. The eastern portion was granted to Malcolm Fraser and the western part, Murray Bay, to John Nairne. The eastern section, three thousand acres which Fraser named Mount Murray, extended from the north shore of the Malbaie River to the Black River and was over three leagues in depth. The western section, three thousand acres of which belonged to Nairne alone, ran from Cap-aux-Oies to the Malbaie River. The river that flowed through the middle marked the boundary between the

Captain John Nairne at Murray Bay, *a watercolour by Charles W. Jefferys, 1929 PAC, C-40592*

*Ancien manoir de la famille Nairne, à la Malbaie (autre vue)*

*Old Nairne family manor house at La Malbaie, circa 1925.*
*Photo: ANQ, 874-327*

two estates and was named Murray River. It is interesting to note that Murray Bay, Mount Murray and Shoolbred in the Gaspé were the only lands granted in fief and seigneury by the British government. Murray Bay, which included the actual village of La Malbaie and Pointe-au-Pic, has kept its name all this time. The locals continued to refer to Mount Murray, however, as Cap-à-l'Aigle, the name Champlain had given it. (Roy, 1895)

The names of these two Scottish officers figure largely in the history of Charlevoix. The descendants of Fraser and Nairne have stayed on. Together with the French who were there before them, and often adopting their language, they built Charlevoix into what it is today.

Although Malcolm Fraser did not spend much time on his seigneury, Nairne developed a taste for the life of the gentleman farmer and decided to live on his estate permanently. He organized the seigneury and built a manor house in which he would raise a family with his wife, Christiana Emery. He became the true seigneur of La Malbaie. The Nairnes often entertained friends from Québec, Montréal and Scotland in their manor house. The role of the new seigneur was basically the same as that of the former French seigneurs in that his primary responsibility was to develop the land and settle tenant farmers on it.

The seigneurs' houses on both estates were elegant and luxurious, and European and Canadian friends were only too happy to visit. Nairne rapidly became a prominent host. He would invite his friends to come and take advantage of the outdoors at La Malbaie – the fishing in particular, as the many rivers were chock full of trout and salmon. He convinced them that this was the ideal place for escaping the cares, and the wear, of the city. It was a hospitable land where the seigneurs' generosity was matched by the kindness and simplicity of the inhabitants.

La Malbaie was not an easy place to get to, however. The only way to make the trip from Québec City or Montréal was by coastal schooner or in one of the vessels owned by the wealthy. The increasing infatuation with nature created by the romanticism movement, however, and the urge to escape the cities when they were at their most unpleas-ant and unhealthy, i.e. in the summertime, made the voyage worth it. In 1832, the cholera epidemic prompted a mass exodus from the cities of families seeking the fresh air of the countryside. From that point on, the key resorts of Gaspé, Kamouraska, Cacouna, Rivière-du-Loup and La Malbaie flourished.

Beginning in 1830, pleasure trips along the St. Lawrence were made possible for the general public. The first vessel to make the run was the *Waterloo*, owned by the St. Lawrence Steamboat Company. Later, the Montréal & Québec Steamship Company's steamships *Rowland Hill* and *Alliance* carried passengers from the cities to their vacation destination twice a week.

Murray Bay, sometimes described as a "beautiful grassy valley on the North Shore," became the most fashionable place to spend one's summer holidays. The residents of La Malbaie were quick to open up their homes to these tourists, who represented an unexpected new source of income. The family of Charlotte Holt Gethings was one of the first to come and spend the summer in Charlevoix. This new social phenomenon was first described in a book by Charlotte Gethings MacPherson entitled *Reminiscences of Old Québec*, which was published in 1890. In her book, the author talks about how the summer vacationers spent their time in Murray Bay in 1840.

*Murray Village, Québec, circa 1895.*
*Photo: McCord Museum of Canadian History, Montreal,*
*Notman Archives, 3286*

*Murray Bay, circa 1930.*
*Photo: S.J. Hayward, CSL coll.*

In 1853, a wharf was built at Pointe-au-Pic and several steamship companies began to organize three-day boat trips, with stops along the St. Lawrence on the way, culminating in a cruise up the Saguenay River. A number of hotels sprouted up to accommodate travelers. Notable families from Montréal, Québec City and Toronto frequented Duberger's Hotel, the Warren Hotel and the Chamard's Lorne House, to name some of the earliest hotels. Among those who came were the Dow, Caverhill, Drummond and Molson families from Montréal; the Sewell, Price, Garneau and Lemesurier families from Québec; and, from Toronto, the family of William Blake, Solicitor General of Upper Canada.

In 1894, huge summer houses began to appear on the Pointe-au-Pic hillside. Some of these houses were designed by architect Harry Stavely of Québec City, Jean-Charles Warren of La Malbaie, and even the firm McKim Mead & White of New York. These summer houses were designed in the very latest styles: the American shingle style, the Norman style, or the British style used in Norman Shaw's country houses. These houses, which were often built by locals, stood out from other homes being built in Québec at the time by virtue of the materials used, their interior décor and their design. All of these wealthy homeowners and their families had an inevitable "snowball" effect and before long La Malbaie became a prestigious resort destination among Canadians on the lookout for sun and saltwater.

*Maxwell drawing*, Hotel at Murray Bay
for the Richelieu & Ontario Nav. Co.
*Ill.: Canadian Architecture Collection,
McGill University*

Bois-de-la-Roche,
*Louis Forget's home
in Senneville.*
*Photo: Canadian Architecture
Collection, McGill University*

# PART I

# The Manoir Richelieu

# THE RICHELIEU &
# ONTARIO NAVIGATION COMPANY

IN THE END, IT WAS THE RICHELIEU & ONTARIO Navigation Company that developed tourism in Pointe-au-Pic and turned it into the most popular resort in Québec.

In 1894, Louis J. Forget became the company's president. He wanted to enhance the stopover experience for passengers on the cruise ships that sailed to Pointe-au-Pic and Tadoussac by offering them a wider range of services. With this in mind, he decided to build a grand hotel on the cliff at Pointe-au-Pic.

In 1898, Forget commissioned Montréal architect Edward Maxwell to design a huge hotel with two hundred and fifty guestrooms. He had sound reasons for choosing Maxwell.

### Edward Maxwell

In 1890, a competition had called for design submissions for the Board of Trade Building in Montréal. Sixteen plans were submitted by Canadian and American firms. The jury, presided over by New York architect Richard Morris Hunt, chose the Shepley, Rutan & Coolidge design. Edward Maxwell was working for this Boston firm at the time and he was put in charge of overseeing the construction work. This brought the architect back to his hometown of Montréal

and, afterwards, he decided to stay on there. The Board of Trade building established Maxwell's reputation in the business world. Several financiers hired him to design hotels, office buildings and homes for them. It was during this period that Maxwell designed a country house for Louis Forget, the man who would later head the Richelieu & Ontario Navigation Company. Forget and his family were thrilled with the magnificent stone house, which they named Bois-de-la-Roche. This summer house on the shores of Lake St. Louis inspired many of the others that sprang up in the area after it. Forget was so impressed with Maxwell's talent that he decided to have him design his hotel in Murray Bay.

In Boston, Edward Maxwell had worked for a firm that had taken over Henry Hobson Richardson's clientele. Richardson is considered to have been one of the most brilliant architects in the United States in the 1870s and 1880s. Although he was not involved in any of it personally, Edward Maxwell was familiar with Richardson's work and he studied his designs and plans with special interest. His impressive and prolific accomplishments included many designs for houses clad in shingles. These shingle-style houses included Ames Gate Lodge, and the Andreas,

Sherman, Codman and Bryant houses. Maxwell also took a special interest in the new architectural style of the summer houses being designed by John Calvin Stevens in Portland, W.R. Emerson and Robert Swaine Peabody in Boston, and McKim Mead and White in New York. In 1879, William Ralph Emerson designed the first country house completely covered in shingles, the C.J. Morrill house on Mount Desert Island. At the time, it was considered a monument of the shingle style.

Edward Maxwell was very interested in the work of American architects promoting the shingle style. He experimented with it himself and was quite successful – at St. Andrews in New Brunswick for example. Because of the growing popularity of the shingle style, he decided to use it for the hotel he was designing for the Richelieu & Ontario Navigation Company. The design for this hotel on the hilltop at Pointe-au-Pic was not unlike the famous Banff Springs Hotel in the Rockies, designed by architect Bruce Price.

The Banff Springs was a palatial wooden structure with high-pitched roofs punctuated by dormer windows and chimneys. Its spacious open verandas were at one with the natural beauty around them. Maxwell worked with architect George Cuttler Shattuck, from the Boston firm of that name, on the design for the hotel at Pointe-au-Pic.

While he was still working on the hotel plans, Maxwell called on Frederick Todd's American landscape architecture firm to design the hotel grounds. Todd's drawing showed the hotel's ground plan with a salt-water swimming pool behind it, tennis courts on the lawns, horseback riding trails and two buildings further back: a stable that was completely covered in shingles and a bowling alley.

# THE FIRST HOTEL:
## A PALATIAL WOODEN STRUCTURE
## OVERLOOKING THE ST. LAWRENCE RIVER

The hotel built by the Richelieu & Ontario Navigation Company opened on June 15, 1899. It was built entirely of wood and it was magnificent – both because it was architecturally imposing and because it was so dramatically set on a cliff overlooking the mighty St. Lawrence. Such an impressive structure deserved a name worthy of its seigneurial roots, and so it was named the Manoir Richelieu.

The hotel designed by Edward Maxwell consisted of a main body flanked by four rectangular towers and a lower wing on each side. Its shingles, its many windows and doors, and its steep-pitched roofs and countless chimneys all combined to give the build-

*Manoir Richelieu in 1899. Photo: Postcard, Donald Dion coll.*

ing a picturesque look. It was a perfect counterpoint to the rugged landscape around it. On the ground floor, a huge circular veranda offered a breathtaking view of the St. Lawrence River and the cliffs of Charlevoix.

The Manoir had two hundred and fifty beautifully decorated guestrooms and adjacent bathrooms equipped with running fresh water and saltwater. The walls of the huge lounges were covered in wooden paneling and the ceilings were beamed. A few pieces of wicker furniture scattered here and there around the capacious, modern chesterfields gave these rooms a summer house air. The large Brussels carpets, which added a hushed elegance to the atmosphere, and the bronze-

Murray Bay, Canada, Manoir Richelieu.

*The circular veranda in 1899.*
*Photo: W. Notman, McCord Museum of Canadian History,*
*Montreal, Notman Archives*

coloured woodwork, the lighting, the exposed beams and the stone fireplaces made for an intimate and refined look.

Every afternoon, for the guests' enjoyment and pleasure, the Manoir's vast lounges came alive with the sounds of an orchestra. After spending a day in the pool or on the tennis courts, the hotel's clients could savour local specialties and European gastronomical delights.

Drawing of Manoir
on a hotel bill.
Donald Dion coll.

Manoir Richelieu interior, circa 1930.
Photo: S.J. Hayward, CSL coll.

*The hotel's first saltwater pool. Photo: S.J. Hayward, CSL coll.*

Most of the tourists came to Charlevoix from Ottawa, Toronto, New York City, Boston, Philadelphia, Montréal and Québec City. Some of them would stay in small hotels or room with local families at Cap-à-l'Aigle, Saint-Irénée and La Malbaie. Little by little, a community of summer visitors grew up around the Manoir. Many enthusiasts of resort life and nature's wonders built summer houses there for their families. For forty years, from 1895 to 1935, William Howard Taft, the 27th president of the United States, spent all of his summers in Charlevoix.

Many important Québecers came to stay with him at Fassifern Cottage: Sir Charles Fitzpatrick, Québec's lieutenant governor; Sir Lomer Gouin, its premier; the chief justice of the Québec Supreme Court, Albert Sévigny; and many influential businessmen from Montréal. During that same period, Rodolphe Forget, a notable Montréal financier, settled on a huge estate in Saint-Irénée, the *Gilmont*. The Burroughs-Pelletier family was one of the first families to settle in Cap-à-l'Aigle. In 1840, John Burroughs spent his first summer there with his daughter, who

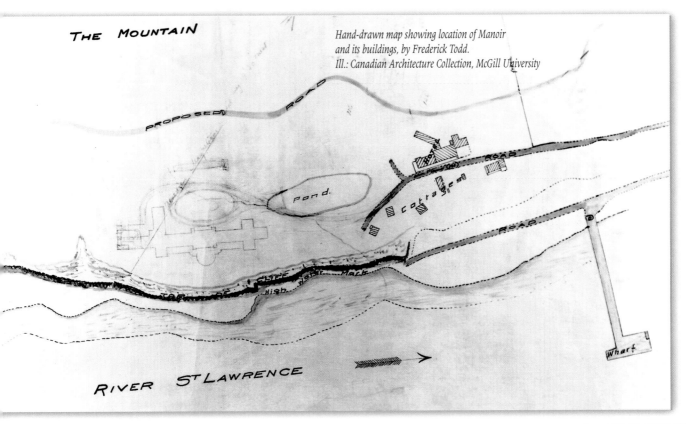

THE MOUNTAIN

*Hand-drawn map showing location of Manoir and its buildings, by Frederick Todd.*
*Ill.: Canadian Architecture Collection, McGill University*

Pond.

Cottages

Wharf

RIVER ST. LAWRENCE

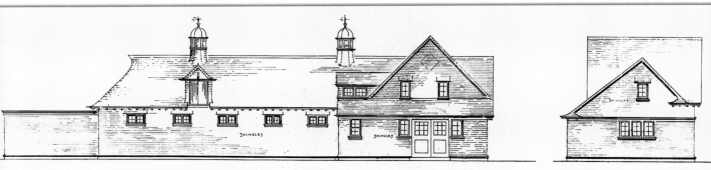

*Drawing of stables by Edward Maxwell.*
*Ill.: Maxwell Collection, Canadian Architecture Collection, McGill University*

*Drawing of bowling alley by Edward Maxwell.*
*Ill.: Maxwell Collection, Canadian Architecture Collection, McGill University*

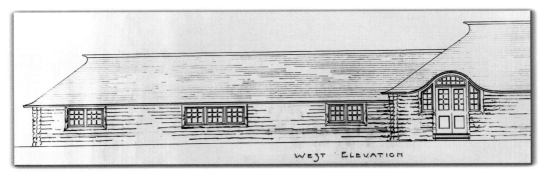

WEST ELEVATION

*Gil'Mont, Rodolphe Forget's*
*house in Saint-Irénée*
*Photo: Maxwell Collection,*
*Canadian Architecture*
*Collection, McGill University*

was married to Elzéard Pelletier. The Burroughs and Pelletiers built *Mont Plaisant*, the *Sorbier* and the *Gite*; the Pelletier family still has their picturesque cottage, the *Sorbier*, in Cap-à-l'Aigle. A small society of affluent summer people was thus created around the Manoir Richelieu, where they built their country houses and cottages. They began going to Charlevoix in 1840 and are still seen there today. (Dubé, 1990)

# THE MANOIR RICHELIEU GOLF CLUB

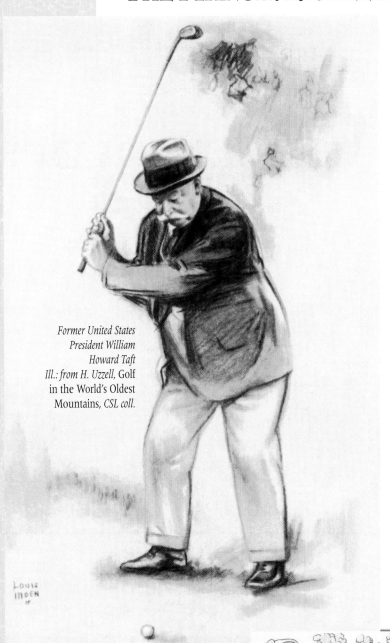

Former United States
President William
Howard Taft
*Ill.: from H. Uzzell,* Golf
in the World's Oldest
Mountains, *CSL coll.*

Pointe-au-Pic quickly became the most fashionable, high-society resort thanks to the Manoir's reputation. With its select client base in mind, the hotel had a golf course built adjoining the course of the Murray Bay Golf Club, which had opened in 1876.

*The scenery surrounding the Manoir Richelieu Golf Course is the most impressive setting for a links of which I have knowledge. The chief task I faced was to build this natural beauty into every possible feature of the play. No designer could have more varied or lavish material to work with. Both play and scenery will, I am sure, prove a delight to every visitor.*

These are the words of Herbert Strong, the architect chosen to design the golf course at the Manoir. Strong had already designed the Inwood, the Engineers on Long Island, and the Lakeview in Toronto, so he was the ideal person for designing a course that would do justice to the awesome panorama of the majestic St. Lawrence and the beautiful Laurentian Mountains.

*The* Trou des fées
*Ill.: from H. Uzzell,*
Golf in the World's Oldest
Mountains, *CSL coll.*

N°9
TROU DES FÉES
330 YDS

TEE

*Uphill tramway, circa 1947.*
*Photo: Max Sauer Jr., CSL coll.*

*Enjoying a round of golf, 1947.*
*Photo: Max Sauer Jr., CSL coll.*

*Clubhouse under construction, 1937. Photo: private coll.*

Work began on the golf course on June 18, 1924, and it opened one year later to the day. William Howard Taft, the former U.S. president and resident of Point-au-Pic, presided over the opening ceremonies. The golf course rapidly became known as one of the most beautiful in the world – sited, as it was, on land that was part of the Pointe-au-Pic forest and what with its incredible view. The greens were named poetically: the *Nordet* on the high ground where the north wind was always keenly felt; *Terrebonne, Cap Noir* and *Trait Carré* after villages in the old seigneury of La Malbaie; *Le Maire,* in honour of the engineer Hector Warren, who had helped design the Murray Bay Golf Course when he was the mayor; *Trou des Fées,* in reference to the legend about gods of the

*Pointe-au-Pic*
*Ill.: C.W. Simpson,*
*France Gagnon*
*Pratte coll.*

mountains in this Valhalla; and, finally, the *Malbaie*, which overlooked the greens and could only be reached by going up zigzagging stairs.

In 1934, the architect David Sheenan designed a clubhouse building inspired by traditional Québec architecture.

*Clubhouse, circa 1947.*
*Photo: Max Sauer Jr., CSL coll.*

*Drawing by Joseph Abrams, circa 1929*
*CSL coll.*

# PART 2

# The Second Manoir

## JOHN S. ARCHIBALD

ON SEPTEMBER 12, 1928, TWENTY-NINE YEARS after it opened, the Manoir Richelieu burned down. The cause of the fire was never found. The very next day, however, the general manager of Canada Steamship Lines, T.R. Enderby, called reporters from the Montréal *Gazette* to inform them that a new hotel would be built on the site. Architect John S. Archbald was commissioned to design it.

---

John S. Archibald

Born in 1872 in Inverness, Scotland, Archibald apprenticed with the Scottish architect William MacIntosh up until 1893. He then moved to Montréal, where he entered the office of Edward Maxwell on Beaver Hall Square as a draftsman. He met Charles J. Saxe there, who was one of the most promising architects in the firm. Armed with all the experience they had acquired working for Maxwell, Saxe and Archibald decided to open up their own office in 1897.

From the very start, the new firm, Saxe & Archibald, was remarkably successful. It began to make a name for itself thanks to a number of hotel projects that it carried out for the Canadian Pacific Railway Company. It designed additions for the Château Laurier in Ottawa, for instance, and drew up the plans for the Hotel Vancouver. The partnership ended in 1915, and Archibald continued to work in his own name. His reputation grew as he designed more and more important buildings, such as the Westmount home of Noah Timmins, and the Masonic Temple, forum and baseball stadium in Montréal.

John S. Archibald was highly regarded by his colleagues and they elected him president of the Royal Architectural Institute of Canada in 1924 and 1925. At that point, he had already been a member of the Province of Quebec Association of Architects and the International Congress of Architects for twenty years. In 1930, he was made a Fellow of the Royal Architectural Institute of Canada.

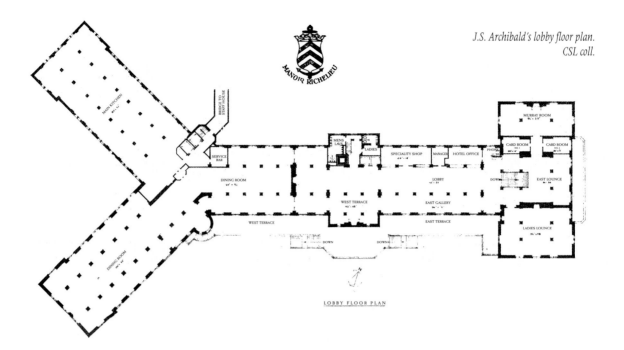

LOBBY FLOOR PLAN

Incline railway used to haul materials up to
the Manoir during its construction.
Photo: CSL coll.

In the September 1930 issue of the *Journal of the Royal Architectural Institute of Canada*, Archibald commented on the challenge of building the Manoir Richelieu, which he had just completed:

*The construction of the Manoir presented some very interesting and difficult problems for the architect and contractor. In the first place, the Canada Steamship Company desired to open the new hotel on June 15th, 1929, approximately eight months after building operations commenced on October 15th, 1928. Secondly, the location was such that careful consideration had to be given to all materials. This involved major difficulties for the site was in the centre of the wilderness, so to speak, some two hundred feet above the level of the wharf and railway siding and ninety miles from Québec, the nearest supply depot. Finally it was decided to build a concrete structure, utilizing, as far as possible, local materials. Plenty of rock could be obtained from the surrounding hills and a crusher was therefore set up supplying all the stone required for the concrete, the only ingredient to be imported being cement. A special incline railway was also built for hauling materials from the wharf and railway up to the site of the building.*

In this article, Archibald also described the interior design in detail:

*The new Manoir is designed and furnished in the picturesque style prevailing in France during the period when Cardinal Richelieu dominated the affairs of that country and the Chateau traditions have been closely followed in the interior arrangements. Entrance to the Manoir is on the grade level through a loggia into the entrance lobby. The floors of this lobby are of travertine and the walls are lined to their full height with Jeanne d'Arc stone brought from France and finished with a black marble base. Grouped around the entrance hall are the tavern, billiard room and various shops. The greater part of this lower floor is occupied by the mechanical and service quarters.*

*The main floor is reached from the entrance lobby by a wide stone staircase with wrought iron balustrade. Leading from the main lobby at the top of the stairs is the east terrace which provides a fine view across the St. Lawrence River. The entrance to the large dining room, which is located in the south-west wing, is through the tower-lounge while the north-west wing is entirely occupied by the main kitchen, bake shop and stores.*

The three spacious lounges leading from the public lobby are an interesting feature of the hotel. The north lounge is known as the Murray Room. It contains a portrait of General Murray placed over a marble fireplace. The Manoir trophies, antiques and a complete Canadiana collection are also lodged there. In the east lounge is placed the St. Lawrence chart which depicts the geographical high lights in early exploration of the Great Lakes and St. Lawrence water highways and covers the period of the French occupation ending with the capitulation in 1759. From the east lounge, one passes to the south lounge which is also known as the ladies' room. This room is very definitely French in tone. The central motif being a portrait of the first lady of New France, Madame Champlain.

*Dormer window with crest. Photo: CSL coll.*

*Building site in winter in its wooden cocoon. Photo: Arnott & Rogers Ltd., CSL coll.*

*End of construction, 1929.*
*Photo: Arnott & Rogers Ltd., CSL coll.*

*The upper floors contain some 300 bedrooms with a vice-regal suite and 15 special suites. The staff quarters in block "E" were so arranged that if they were required they could be turned into typical bedrooms; this has since been done and a new staff house and garage has been built at the rear of the property.*

*Connected to the hotel by a covered cloister and some 150 feet distant is the open air swimming pool and casino, which was inspired by the Chateau de Ramezay. The casino is equipped in the basement with dressing room facilities for the bathers and the main floor for dancing and moving picture entertainment. The pool is an open air one of regular dimensions, with heated re-circulated salt water and lounging and spectators' benches surrounding it, protected by trelliswork from cold wind.*

Archibald called upon the Toronto contractors Wilde & Bryden for the construction of the Manoir, a building that would measure 425 feet by 52 feet and stand in the middle of 430 acres. A thousand construction workers, divided into two shifts, began work on the hotel in October. They excavated the site with pickaxes and shovels, digging 20 feet deep. They then built a wooden

"shell," or cocoon, around a frame: the construction work would be done inside this cocoon. This procedure had proved very effective during the 1925 reconstruction of the Château Lake Louise hotel in the Rockies, overseen by the architect William Painter. *Construction* magazine, with a large circulation in Canada and the United States, had helped spread the good news of this innovative procedure that made it possible to build in the wintertime. The temperature inside the cocoon was kept high enough to protect the construction materials and workers.

Inside this shell, a phenomenal amount of concrete was poured into a wooden bedding for the foundation. The walls were put up the same way, at a rate of one floor a week. All these concrete walls were brushed with steel to give them a rough, stone-like finish. The floors, walls and divisions were made of concrete poured into wooden

*The casino adjacent
to the pool.
Photo: Max Sauer
Studio, CSL coll.*

*The new saltwater pool.
Photo: CSL coll.*

moulds and the roof was made of aerated concrete clad with copper. The only part of the structure that was built separately was the large dormer window in the west wall bearing the hotel's coat of arms, which was added and connected to the building with steel girders. Archibald had white marble laid on the concrete floors of the ground floor and terrazzo on the lobby floor. Both sides of the lobby on the main floor featured an archway, creating a nave and side aisles which were lit by twelve bay windows. On the south side, these bay windows opened out onto terraces overlooking the river. The nave gave onto a lounge with an immense fireplace.

The casino was also built at the same time – at a distance of 150 feet from the Manoir. This concrete building designed by

*The building is unveiled on June 15, 1929.*
*Photo: Associated Screen News Ltd., CSL coll.*

John S. Archibald drew its inspiration from the Château Ramezay in Montréal, with its towers in the façade and its majestic entrance. It had a huge room completely finished in British Columbia fir, with exposed beams. The casino was where dances were held and also where moving pictures were shown. Large French doors opened out onto a terrace overlooking the swimming pool, a popular venue among summer guests.

Eaton's and Simpson's of Canada were entrusted with the interior decoration of the Manoir.

With the removal of its temporary outer shell, the hotel was at last unveiled, as was the building behind it for the Manoir's 450 employees. The official opening took place on June 15, 1929.

# A Château on High

The Manoir looked like a majestic Norman château, standing out dramatically on its cliff against the backdrop of the sky. Its many towers and turrets relieved the building's austerity and its steep copper roofs added a picturesque touch. It was very important to the steamship company that the new hotel be fireproof. This is why rough concrete was used throughout, making for very plain, smooth walls. The façade was enhanced, however, by countless windows, doors and large verandas, and various architectural elements alleviated the severity of the walls. There was a grand entrance portico, for example, as well as François I hanging dormers, high chimneys and several recesses in the façade.

*Main lobby
in 1930.
Photo: Hayward
Studios, CSL coll.*

*Large fireplace
in lobby.
Photo: Hayward
Studios, CSL coll.*

*The luxurious
interiors of the
Manoir Richelieu,
circa 1930.
Photo: S.J. Hayward,
CSL coll.*

Guests entering through the high portico were immediately struck by the lavish interiors. A monumental staircase led from the entrance up to the main lobby, where a series of large halls were set between the two huge arches. These halls ended in a lounge featuring a high fireplace decorated with the coat of arms of Cardinal Richelieu. Beyond the arches, large French windows opened onto vast glassed-in terraces offering a spectacular view of the dramatic Charlevoix landscape. The west end of the long rectangular building was terminated by two Y-shaped wings. In one of them was the grand dining room, which was entirely decorated with John James Audubon's four hundred and thirty-five ornithological works from *The Birds of America*. The other wing held ultra-modern kitchens. In addition, there was the sumptuously decorated Pink Lounge for the ladies, which featured a large painting by Sheriff Scott, *Madame de Champlain Teaching the Indian Children*, as well as the Murray Room, a smoking room finished

*Cardinal Richelieu
in the main lobby
Photo: From a
publicity brochure,
CSL coll.*

*Audubon prints in
the dining room
Photo: From a
publicity brochure,
CSL coll.*

*Lobby.*
*Photo: S.J. Hayward,*
*CSL coll.*

with bronze-coloured woodwork. The whole floor had been designed to delight the eye.

It was largely the refinement and elegance of its interior décor that earned the new Manoir Richelieu its reputation as the most luxurious hotel in the country. This success was partly attributable to the president of the Canada Steamship Lines, William Hugh Coverdale, who personally put together the collection of engravings, paintings, carpets, antique maps and art imported from France, complemented by Québec crafts, on display in the hotel. The collection was added to the tapestries and huge historical paintings on the walls of the hotel's vast rooms, which included *The Seigneur of La Malbaie*, by Charles W. Jefferys, *Christopher Columbus at the Court of Ferdinand and Isabella*, by Wenceslas de Brozik, *Captain John Nairne Landing at Murray Bay*, by Charles W. Jefferys, and last but not least *Portrait of Brigadier General James Murray*, by Adam Sherriff Scott. The collection contained a total of three thousand pieces amassed by William Hugh Coverdale between 1929 and 1949, and the new hotel was the guardian of them all! Now, all of the paintings, with the exception of five of them, are conserved at the Public Archives of Canada in Ottawa.

Christopher Columbus at the Court of Ferdinand and Isabella, *painting by Wenceslas de Brozik, from the Manoir's Coverdale collection. Photo: CSL coll.*

The interior decoration, from the grand halls to the charming guestrooms with their slanted ceilings, reflected the hotel's association with Charlevoix and with the motherland, France. The maps of New France, historical portraits of French notables, watercolour paintings of the region, wrought-iron fixtures imported from Germany and Austria, French pier glasses, Louis XV furniture in the lounges and bedrooms, and the silk and Jouy prints embellishing the walls all combined to remind the beholder that the Manoir Richelieu was on French Canadian soil.

The three hundred and fifty guestrooms were furnished in the French style and decorated with flowered carpets that created a country atmosphere. There were dormer windows in the rooms on the top floor, right under the high-pitched copper roofs. The hotel also offered several suites for important guests and for the owners from Canada Steamship Lines. The refined, sumptuous interior decoration and impeccable European-style service attracted countless wealthy Canadians and Americans in search of luxury as well as outdoor activities. Like former U.S. president William Taft, many of them were seduced by the charm of what they referred to as Canada's Newport and built themselves lovely houses in the area. Among these were the Bienvenue, Garneau, Forget and Fish families, and the Cabots, Minturns, Chapins, Bancrofts, Dempseys, Bonners, McCaggs, Kings, Kennedys, Morgans, Boardmans, Ryans, Livingwoods, Warrens, Blakes, Fitzpatricks, Bennets and Donahues.

The Murray Room:
for gentlemen only.
Photo: Hayward
Studios, CSL coll.

A period
guestroom.
Photo: CSL coll.

*Publicity promoting activities at the Manoir in the fifties.*
*Ill.: C. Lampari, CSL coll.*

# THE GOOD LIFE

The elegant décor was further enhanced by the often extravagant activities of wealthy, young and athletic guests. They would reserve suites for the whole summer or for several weeks of vacation. Some of them would bring their children – the youngest of whom would be accompanied by a nurse. All these lucky people were busy amusing themselves and taking part in all sorts of entertainments and sports activities from morning until nighttime.

At daybreak, they were served breakfast in their suites or on the huge outdoor terrace by the well-trained hotel staff. Then it would be time to get a little exercise. The Manoir had its own horseback riding trails and riding masters to accompany parents and children. Once they had returned from their ride or their

tennis or lawn bowling, a refreshing swim in the enormous saltwater pool in front of the hotel would beckon. At noontime, the hotel orchestra would start playing on the casino terrace adjacent to the pool as guests watched the antics of swimmers while enjoying a drink before lunch. This pool was a favourite meeting place for all the summer people of Pointe-au-Pic, so a sandy beach, called the *Lido,* was added for everyone's enjoyment.

*The Manoir terrace on the river side. Photo: CSL coll.*

*Lawn bowling. Photo: Associated Screen News Ltd., CSL coll.*

Live music for bathers
and spectators alike.
Photo: Max Sauer, CSL coll.

Putting
green close to
the Manoir.
Photo: CSL coll.

Manoir Richelieu
Golf Club Shield,
the annual
tournament trophy.
Photo: Associated
Screen News Ltd.,
CSL coll.

The elegantly dressed guests had their luncheon on the Manoir terrace, with its view of the rugged Charlevoix landscape and the St. Lawrence, as they chatted about how they would spend their afternoon. The latest sports equipment and facilities were placed at the disposal of these distinguished people. Golf and tennis were the most popular sports. The Manoir Richelieu and Murray Bay golf clubs and their members competed at tournaments throughout the summer. Golfers would often lunch on the clubhouse terrace before going back for another nine holes. The fate of many a political party, bank and company was decided on these beautiful greens over a game of golf. All of the golfers coveted the famous hotel trophy, the Manoir Richelieu Golf Club Shield, and the award festivities were truly memorable.

*Miss Taft diving.
Photo: Jules Blouin,
CSL coll.*

*Horseback riding
at the Manoir.
Photo:
Jules Blouin,
CSL coll.*

*Fun and games
at the pool.
Photo: Max Sauer,
CSL coll.*

*Fashion show.*
*Photo: CSL coll.*

*Annual dog show. Photo: CSL coll.*

*Tennis tournament*
*in the sixties.*
*Photo: Jules Blouin,*
*CSL coll.*

*Hélène Cannon
personifying the forest
at a costume party.
Photo: CSL coll.*

Tennis competitions were also organized every week, much to the enjoyment of players from Québec, Montréal and Toronto. Come Saturday night, the trophies would be handed out at a lively reception.

Towards the middle of the afternoon, entertainment was organized for hotel guests as well as people spending the summer in the area, who were only too happy to temporarily abandon their fine country houses and head for the Manoir lawns. Ensconced in the shade and amply provided with such creature comforts as drinks and refreshments, this sophisticated elite would join in carefully selected activities. Dog shows were popular, for example. They gave people a chance to see the Manoir guests parade their pedigree pets and to guess who would win the trophy. The next day, it might be the children's turn to take part in a fashion show featuring clothing and knits made by people from La Malbaie. Sometimes, models would even show off luxurious furs created by Canadian fashion designers. Needless to say, the children's costume parties always drew a crowd of enthusiastic parents and friends. There were also sporting events, such as archery contests and lawn

*Archery contest on the lawn.
Photo: CSL coll.*

*The wharf at
La Malbaie in 1934.
Photo: CNR coll.*

*View of the "white ships"
from the Manoir.
Photo: Max Sauer, CSL coll.*

*Passing the time on the terrace, 1934.*
*Photo: Associated Screen News Ltd., CSL coll.*

bowling competitions. Many of these activities were organized to raise funds for charities, for example the huge Red Cross bazaar held every summer at Cap-à-l'Aigle and at the Manoir.

One special event every Thursday inevitably turned out to be the attraction of the day: the arrival at the Pointe-au-Pic wharf of the impressive white steamers of Canada Steamship Lines. By 1927, a flotilla of ships specially designed for trips along the St. Lawrence and Saguenay rivers flew the steamship company's red and black flag. These boats, referred to as the "white ships," were the last word in river steamers. They would leave Victoria Pier, in Montréal, at

seven o'clock in the morning, after boarding Canadian and American passengers who made their way to Montréal by train, bus or car. These well-to-do people often traveled with their superb cars, which were stowed on the lower decks. The steamers eventually plied the St. Lawrence from the Great Lakes to the Saguenay, offering a variety of cruises designed for affluent passengers. By 1947, for instance, the company had five trips to the Saguenay to choose from: four departing either

*Overlooking the river.*
*Photo: CSL coll.*

CATALOGUE OF CHARGES

The
Manoir Richelieu
Pointe-au-Pic, P.Q.
(Murray Bay)

SEASON JUNE TO SEPTEMBER

1958

*Owned and Operated by*
CANADA STEAMSHIP LINES

from Detroit, Buffalo, Toronto or Montréal, and the famous "Richelieu Cruise" that took passengers past Capes Trinity and Eternity all the way to Chicoutimi. This six-day cruise from Montréal, which cost $72.50, was especially popular. It included sightseeing in Québec City, Tadoussac and Chicoutimi, one day and an evening at the Manoir Richelieu, and side trips on the way back to St. Anne de Beaupré and Montmorency Falls.

*Ill.: From cruise publicity, coll. CSL*

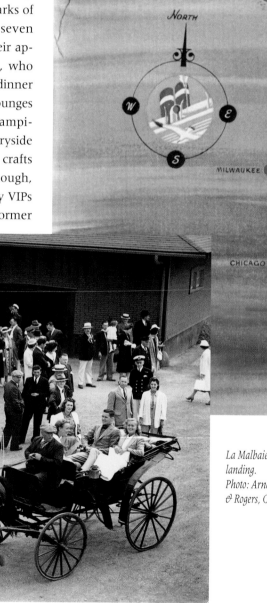

When night fell, the brightly-lit Manoir shone in its glorious Charlevoix setting overlooking the St. Lawrence. At five o'clock in the afternoon, after teatime in the Pink Lounge, the "ladies" would retire to their rooms to "freshen up" and don their evening atire with the help of the chambermaids. Breathtaking gowns created by Parisian *couturiers* and New York designers, splendid jewellery, daring hairdos – these were the hallmarks of these elegant summer visitors. At seven o'clock, they would begin to make their appearance, on the arm of their escorts, who would also be very chic in their white dinner jackets. First, they would meet in the lounges and chat about a tennis or golf championship, or about a trip into the countryside to scout out woven cloth *catalognes*, crafts and woolen blankets. In particular, though, they would comment discreetly on any VIPs who might be there that evening – former

*La Malbaie landing.*
*Photo: Arnott & Rogers, CSL coll.*

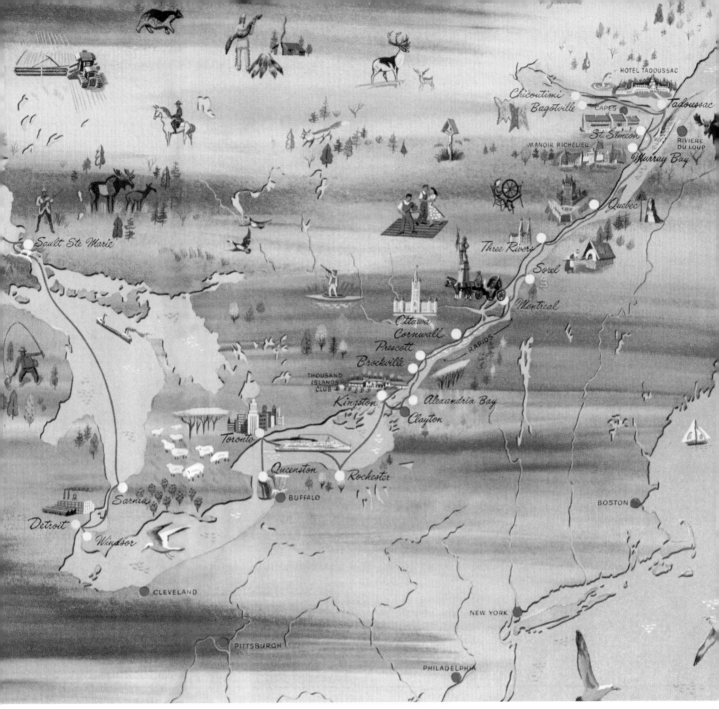

U.S. president William Taft, for example, Hollywood stars such as Fred Astaire, Bob Hope or Bing Crosby, or golf champions coveting the Manoir Richelieu Golf Club Shield. These people were among friends: they were all part of a small colony. Attorneys and businessmen from Montréal, Québec City and Toronto rubbed shoulders with the Americans who frequented the Manoir – the Tafts, McGraths and Graves from Virginia, the Fish family from Washington, and the Thébauds and Robbs from New York. There was also the Kennedy family, which would leave London, England and head for the shores of the St. Lawrence every year.

*From "Your Water Playground," a 1948 publicity brochure Ill.: CSL coll.*

*Splendid view
of the Manoir
upon arrival.
Photo: Arnott
& Rogers, CSL coll.*

*Cocktails in
the lounge
Photo: From
a publicity
brochure*

*A dance in the casino building.*
*Photo: Arnott & Rogers, CSL coll.*

# FISHING IN CHARLEVOIX

For many of these vacationers, fishing was their favourite pastime. Right from the start, when Fraser Highlander officers Fraser and Nairne first set foot in Charlevoix in 1761, fishing enthusiasts had begun to flock to the area. Initially, the seigneur had invited them there, but then they got into the habit of returning every year with their wives and children and eventually ended up building their own cottages or country houses. Some of these houses were quite luxurious and would recreate the atmosphere of their city homes, with a cortege of servants including a nurse for the children, a cook, lady's maid, butler and chauffeur. While the men were off salmon fishing, their families would take the opportunity to bathe in the saltwater or go for walks in the countryside. The fishermen would stay in groups in small, isolated fishing camps on the shores of lakes full of fish. In 1899, the brand new Manoir Richelieu became a popular retreat for these nature lovers and Canada Steamship Lines offered to take them to special fishing camps, complete with guides, porters and cooks.

*Gone fishing*
*Photo: CSL coll.*

*Entrance to the fishing lakes.*
*Photo: CSL coll.*

*Lake Boulanger fishing camp*
*owned by Hôtel Tadoussac.*
*Photo: S.J. Hayward, CSL coll.*

From then on, the Manoir advertising consistently included information about fishing trips to these camps built inland from La Malbaie, in the vicinity of Sagard and Tadoussac. The company had fishing camps near backwoods lakes with names like Comporté, Morin, Gravel, Jacob, Big Lake and Small Lake. The first nature park in Québec had been created in 1894, in fact, to protect the fish. By 1914, there were over two hundred hunting and fishing clubs in the province. When all the private clubs were abolished, there were two thousand of them. To name a few of these clubs, there were the Petite Malbaie, Roche, Chaudière, Prémisse, Bonne Veine, Tourelli and Triton. Manoir guests were driven to the park entrance by car, where they were taken in hand and accommodated in rustic camps. These camps were their base and they would explore the rivers and lakes around them. This fishing trip tradition, which has lived on to this day, played a major part in the popularity of the Manoir Richelieu.

# Snowy Weather

Although originally designed as a summer resort, in 1930 the Manoir opened its doors for the winter season for the first time. A widespread advertising campaign had vaunted the merits of winter sports and activities in the Charlevoix region in order to draw as many visitors as possible. Here is an excerpt from one of the brochures:

> You will revel in the luxurious hospitality of the Manoir Richelieu after a long day in the open. Indoors, there is supreme comfort, wonderful meals and jolly companionship. At the door lies the greatest snow country in Eastern Canada.

A weekend at the Manoir Richelieu, including the Pullman train fare, transportation to the hotel, a room and all meals, was offered for a mere $38.85 a day! For $63, guests could spend the whole week there. Among other things, these packages included all the equipment and facilities one could possibly need to take full advantage of Québec's winter.

Preparations for the winter opening slated for mid-December kept all the hotel staff and some of the people from La Malbaie very busy. Woodcutters went to work on the mountain in order to clear the way for a long bobsleigh run all the way back to the Manoir. A ski jump was built as well as several ski trails with evocative names like the Timber Wolf Trail, Red Birds Trail, Bridle Path, Sam Cliff Climb, Birch Trail, Log Roll and the Intercollegiate. A skating rink completed the outdoor picture, while indoors a curling rink and a volleyball court were added to the casino building. The stables were made ready to accommodate horses and sled dogs; sleighs generously outfitted with fur pelts waited for the guests to arrive. Finally, a new club was born: the Timber Wolves Ski Club.

*Manoir Richelieu advertisement in the Montréal* Gazette *CSL coll.*

*Woodcutters at work.*
*Photo: CSL coll.*

*Map of the*
*bobsleigh run*
*and ski trails.*
*CSL coll.*

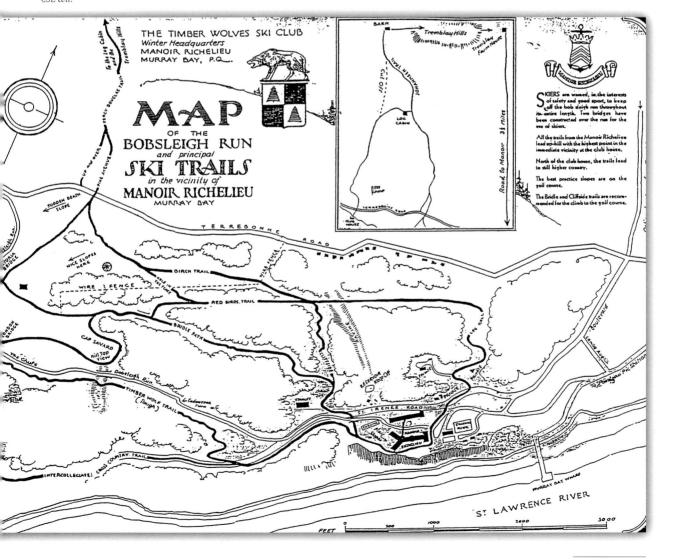

*Curling enthusiasts.*
*Photo: S.J. Hayward Studios, CSL coll.*

The winter season began with the Christmas holidays, and the twinkling decorations and winter mantle of snow gave the hotel a truly magical look in its winter wonderland setting. From December 18, 1929 to February 28, 1930, the guests tasted the joys that winter had to offer at the Manoir, going on ski outings in the hills around La Malbaie, wildly rushing down the bobsleigh run, trying out dogsled rides, skijoring in the valley, and figure skating or playing hockey on the skating rink. Last but not least, there was the event of the season: a ski marathon between Montréal and the Manoir Richelieu.

*Famous ski hike between Montréal and La Malbaie. Photo: S.J. Hayward Studios, CSL coll.*

*Children taking advantage of the joys of winter. Photo: Associated Screen News Ltd., CSL coll.*

*Bobsleighing right up to the door.*
*Photo: Associated Screen News Ltd., CSL coll.*

The hotel's guests appreciated the fine dining and dancing to the sounds of the most popular orchestras and bands of the day. In this setting, which was like something out of a dream, the Christmas and New Year's festivities were unforgettable. However, although the guests were enchanted with their stay, the experience was not exactly a successful one from the hotel's standpoint and the winter season experiment was soon dropped. This failure was partly due to the fact that the great distance between the Manoir and major cities represented an obstacle to tourists in the wintertime and partly to the depression.

*Dogsled trail high over the St. Lawrence. Photo: S.J. Hayward Studios, CSL coll.*

# PART 3

# Hard Times

AFTER THIRTY YEARS, FINANCIAL DIFFICULTIES finally put an end to the success story of the Manoir Richelieu. In 1966, Canada Steamship Lines abandoned its cruises to La Malbaie and the Saguenay. Two years later, it sold the Manoir Richelieu to Warnock Hersey International.

On April 20, 1972, John B. Dempsey, whose family had kept a home in Pointe-au-Pic for a long time, formed the company Manoir Richelieu Limited, which purchased the hotel from Warnock Hersey International. John Dempsey, who was president of the Canadian Enterprise Corporation in Cleveland, formed a partnership with Frank J. Irving and Jacques Dussault of Toronto, who was also a Pointe-au-Pic resident. For three years, Dempsey worked hard to breathe new life into the hotel. In the Murray Bay newsletter *Current Events*, he wrote: "We know there is business validity to the Manoir, its cottages, its golf course and other facilities when managed in a competent manner by those of proven ability in the luxury resort field." In this article, entitled "The Manoir Thrives under New Ownership," he described the key changes he planned to make to the hotel operation in order to revitalize the legendary Pointe-au-Pic hotel.

The season would be extended to the month of October and the former management and support staff would be rehired, since they were familiar with the lifestyle and whims of the clientele concerned. Golf and tennis tournaments would be added to the existing activities and a grand ball would celebrate the end of Golf Week. The hotel hired the Arys Nalbandian Orchestra to play at its dances, which were held every night, and the famous Peter Duchins Rock Band was engaged for the ball. All sorts of improvements were made to the facilities, some of which were designed to allow the hotel to open for extended periods during the winter. But the financial status of the new company deteriorated rapidly, forcing it to declare bankruptcy in July 1975, a few months after the Canadian Pacific Railway Company had been asked to run the hotel.

On December 8, 1975, the *Montreal Star* and Québec City's *Le Soleil* reported that Québec premier Robert Bourassa had announced that the government had decided to buy the Manoir Richelieu in order to help it give a boost to the tourist industry in Charlevoix. The sale price of $950,000 included the hotel, five cottages, the pool and casino building, the eighteen-hole golf course, the tennis courts, the horseback riding and hiking trails and a fishing camp. Bourassa also mentioned the possibility of opening a gambling casino on the Manoir's property. He explained that the Québec government

John Dempsey.
*Photo:* Current Events,
*private coll.*

*Arys Nalbadian.*
*Photo:* Current
Events,
*private coll.*

would not be running the hotel and that this task would be left up to a hotel business. First it was managed by Auberge des Gouverneurs, then by the Dufour family of Île-aux-Coudres from 1983 to 1985.

On April 16, 1986, the government sold the Manoir Richelieu to the Groupe Famille Malenfant, which ran it from 1986 to 1993. The new owner attempted to return the hotel to its former glory by offering new services and redecorating, but this did not work. Relations between hotel management and staff

were strained and repetitive strikes degenerated into a never-ending labour dispute that forced the Groupe Famille Malenfant into bankruptcy.

In 1993, the Fédération des Caisses populaires Desjardins du Québec, the hotel's mortgagee, seized the Manoir Richelieu and then sold it, on December 23 of the same year, to a group of businesspeople that included the architect Michel Côté, Yvan Côté, André Lagacé and Georges Morel.

Michel Côté took on the destiny of the Manoir Richelieu and developed a long-term project to revive the hotel and create a popular resort for the local, Canada-wide and, last but not least, American client base. The ultimate goal was to establish a luxury hotel serving European tourists who would be attracted by the Manoir's reputation for excellence, the beauty of its surroundings, its new casino, upgraded summer vacation activities and renewed winter activities such as skiing, hiking and dogsledding. Special emphasis

*Interior from Groupe Famille Malenfant period.*
*Photo: postcards, CSL coll.*

*Interior from Groupe Famille Malenfant period. Photo: postcards, CSL coll.*

was to be placed on the Europeans' new "thing": snowmobiling. With this in mind, Côté purchased an entire fleet of snowmobiles to place at the guests' disposal.

First of all, Côté ensured Loto-Québec's involvement by installing a casino in the pool building. This casino was linked to the Manoir by an underground passageway. The gambling establishment was an overnight success, bringing in a stable new clientele for the hotel complex. In order to hang on to all of these new clients, Côté had all of the hotel guestrooms and lounges renovated and restored, reinstating the Manoir's tradition of hotel and dining excellence. What is more, he had a fully equipped spa added that included pools, gymnasiums and health care treatment.

For five years, the Manoir Richelieu returned to life and was booked solid summer and winter alike. The local client base was won over first and advertising soon drew Canadian visitors from the other provinces as well as Americans. In 1998, after five years of successful operation, Michel Côté began to plan for the grand hotel's future. He had a vision: he hoped to turn it into a popular world-class resort. This could not be achieved without the help of a sizable financial contribution and an enthusiastic partner, however. After several unsuccessful attempts, Côté saw that the Manoir Richelieu had owners that were in a position to make his international vision come true: he sold the hotel and all its property to a consortium composed of Canadian Pacific Hotels, Loto-Québec, and the Fonds des travailleurs du Québec.

*Drawing of the Charlevoix Casino*
*Ill.: ARCOP/Bernard & Cloutier architectes*

# *Sleeping Beauty Awakes*

IN JUNE OF 1988, CANADIAN PACIFIC HOTELS made a widely publicized announcement, under the heading "Sleeping Beauty Awakes," that it was purchasing the Manoir Richelieu in a consortium with Loto-Québec and the Fonds de solidarité des travailleurs du Québec. They planned to renovate and expand the Manoir and casino from top to bottom, at a cost of $140 million. The grand opening was slated for the famous hotel's hundredth birthday, in June 1999.

According to Alex Kassatly, who was to be the general manager of the revamped hotel: "The renovation and expansion project of Manoir Richelieu will provide the luxury hotel with a splendor reminiscent of its original vocation." Finally, the magnificent Charlevoix hotel would become a world-class hotel by joining the ranks of Canadian Pacific's stately château-style hotels – the Château Frontenac, Château Lake Louise and Banff Springs Hotel.

The renovation and enlargement of both the hotel and the casino began in the early fall of 1998. The architect charged with the reconstruction of the Manoir Richelieu was Bruce Allen, of Le Groupe Arcop, who brought the architectural firm Bernard & Cloutier on board.

*Drawing of the new Manoir.*
*Ill.: ARCOP/Bernard & Cloutier architectes*

*Hotel exterior on St. Lawrence side in 1999.*
*Photo: France Gagnon Pratte*

Bruce Allan comments on the reincarnation of the grand old hotel:

> Between 1970 and 1998, there were several owners who tried to pick up where Canada Steamship Lines had left off, without much success. Gradually, the infrastructure deteriorated, while ill-advised, patch-work efforts at redecoration and reinvigoration only served to make the hotel dowdy and tacky.

> Original and irreplaceable quarter-cut oak furnishings were sold off and trite baroque decoration themes were introduced into the originally simple interior. A 'ballroom' was built at one end of the building in a naïve manner which pretended to reproduce the arcaded expression of the original public spaces but only demonstrated a complete lack of understanding of the architectural language to which it tried to relate.

The additions designed by Bruce Allan and Bernard & Cloutier fit in perfectly with the original style and represented a return to the decorative spirit of the hotel's early years. Major construction work was to be undertaken to provide four hundred luxurious guest rooms – often using three rooms to make two more spacious ones – with washrooms decorated in the thirties style as well as contemporary back-of-the-house services and facilities: staff services, kitchens, deliveries and storage, garbage management, maintenance and administrative areas. The architects also designed a new ballroom that would take up one thousand square metres as well as an underground parking lot for one hundred and fifty cars. The new ballroom would be on the same floor as the lobby, beside a pre-function space looking out onto roof gardens over the garages.

The outside walls would get special treatment. Those of the ballroom were to be clad in sand-blasted precast concrete using aggregate similar to that of the original poured concrete walls. The new dormer windows were designed to recall the old ones, although in a subtly different fashion with contemporary cap details and decorative elements. In the building designed in 1929, the lobby windows looking out towards the St. Lawrence were closed and did not did not allow access to the hotel lawns. This meant that the lobby was completely cut off from the beautiful grounds and gardens with their magnificent views. To alleviate this shortcoming, large French doors were installed this time which opened out onto the terraces and, from there by way of stairs, to the grounds. The wrought-iron balustrades resembled those used in the past.

*Construction site as seen*
*from the back of the hotel in 1999.*
*Photo: France Gagnon Pratte*

Bruce Allan designed a huge glass and metal marquee to be installed at the entrance to the Manoir. Also, in order to give the stark building designed in the thirties something of a facelift, they added suspended lanterns and decorative balconies.

Allan pointed out that by drawing his inspiration from the château style, Archibald had already placed the hotel in the tradition of the Canadian Pacific's famous château-style hotels in 1929. He added that it was interesting that it took so long for the Manoir Richelieu to actually become one of the Canadian Pacific hotel chain's stars – another jewel in its crown.

# THE HEIGHT
# OF REFINED ELEGANCE

In this completely revamped grand hotel, decoration played a key role. The renovations by the architects, who were ever mindful of incorporating volumes, mass, materials and space, had made for a perfectly cohesive whole. It was essential that the interiors reflect this preoccupation with harmony.

The New York City firm Alexandra Champalimaud & Associates (ACA) was entrusted with the interior decoration of the Manoir and its other buildings. Born in Lisbon, where she studied interior design at the Fundaçao Ricardo Espirito Santo Silva, Alexandra Champalimaud moved to Montréal in 1974. She began her career working for Mitchell Holland Ltd. and then formed her own company. Although she lives in Manhattan now, Champalimaud still works in Québec fairly often and is very familiar with Québec's history and old architecture. In fact, she was a member of the Commission des biens culturels from 1986 to 1989. She is renowned for her long-lived interest in historic buildings and her respect for heritage in general. Her firm has built up an international reputation for quality restorations and an original and historically scrupulous style. She has left her mark on the Château Frontenac in Québec City, the extraordinary Algonquin Hotel and Drake Swissôtel in New York, as well as the Ritz-Carlton Rancho Mirage in California and Inter-Continental Hotels in Buenos Aires, Sao Paulo, Paris and Montréal.

In a magazine interview, Alexandra Champalimaud once commented on what she considers to be the key to success with restoration: "Scale, with regard to architecture and interior design." Regarding her working methods, she said: "I make it a point to study a culture and understand its dynamics." Thanks to this meticulous research, the Manoir Richelieu was able to recover the style that had made it one of the most prestigious hotels in North America for so many years.

First of all, Champalimaud studied the hotel's history and original architecture and interior design so that she could recreate the special charm that Coverdale had bestowed upon it. She devoted special attention to finishes and detailing when choosing furniture, fabrics and art. Her decoration reproduces the 1929 atmosphere of the Manoir perfectly. Alexandra Champalimaud explained what was involved in her design description as follows:

*As all the spaces on the Mezzanine level flow into one another, selection of floor coverings, fabrics and wall coverings was essential to ensure gentle transition from one space to another while allowing each individual area to maintain its own identity. The overall scale and proportion of the Mezzanine level dictated materials that reflected the grandness of the space. ACA chose a dark stained oak as the primary material for the wall paneling and furniture throughout the Mezzanine level to reflect the turn of the century Jacobean & Tudor styles.*

The lounges kept their original uses. The men's lounge or cigar room, with its "clubby look," was a replica of the old Murray

*The new interiors reproduce
the original atmosphere. Photo: MR*

Room. ACA gave the former Pink Lounge, or ladies' tea room, a new look in light, sunny tones. All of the restaurants and lounges were given breathtaking views of the hotel's beautiful natural environment. The huge original paintings, French mirrors, bronzes and wrought iron, a remarkable new collection of old maps and charts, period engravings, historical watercolours and, last but not least, a series of old photographs portraying the hotel's hundred years in existence were incorporated into these new interiors. This recreation of the spirit of the Manoir's original interior decoration from Coverdale's day has given the hotel a special historical charm and yet it is also equipped with the latest in sophisticated facilities.

*Fine dining at the Manoir.*
*Photo: MR*

*The new Spa to the west of the hotel.*
*Photo: MR*

A major new addition to the hotel was a spa behind the hotel, complete with two heated saltwater swimming pools to replace the large casino pool. There is also a new convention centre that adds twenty-two thousand feet of space for meetings and a ballroom featuring the impressive Brozic painting *Christopher Columbus at the Court of Ferdinand and Isabella*. This building looks out onto a flower-filled terrace, or roof garden, over the garages.

*Some examples of the beautiful interior
decoration of the Manoir Richelieu.
Photos: François Rivard*

# A CASINO FOR CHARLEVOIX

The casino, a small concrete building adjacent to the pool, in front of the hotel, was generally used for dances and to show movies. Canada Steamship Lines had referred to it as "the casino" even though there had never been any gambling there. The building must have been predestined because in 1975, the Manoir obtained a casino permit from the Québec government.

The architects' firms Gauthier, Guité, Roy and Bernard & Cloutier were retained for the recent renovation and enlargement of the casino. Paul Gauthier describes the project:

*[translation]*

*For a long time, the Charlevoix business community had hoped to open a casino in the region in order to strengthen and extend the tourist season. The enchanting site of the Manoir Richelieu ended up being chosen for this mission. The Société des casinos then decided to renovate and add to an existing building next to the hotel*

*An impressive casino for gambling enthusiasts.*
*Photo: François Rivard*

which had been used as a summer theatre for the past few years and which housed pool facilities on its ground floor.

Although the idea of designing a casino in this exceptional world-renowned location was very appealing to us as architects, we embarked upon the project very cautiously. This architectural complex, the pride and joy of Charlevoix, demanded "soft" intervention that respected its integrity. It would be no small feat to create the extravagant magical atmosphere that one expects to find in a casino, while preserving the romantic spirit of a Victorian building, adapt it to its new vocation, and ensure its harmonious integration as part of a popular and renowned resort complex.

We therefore set ourselves the objective of respecting the building's character by carefully restoring the elements to be conserved and adapting and integrating our additions, which would be contemporary, with the existing structure. The work, which was to be carried out in two phases, included the renovation of the existing building and the addition of enough space to more or less quadruple the volume. Our first challenge was to make sure that the original building's scale remained intact. Another difficulty encountered during the first phase was the problem of incorporating the highly sophisticated technology a casino needs into a building that obviously had not been designed for this purpose. The exceptional air-conditioning load, control measures, electronic wiring connecting all the games to computer consoles, and the omnipresent surveillance cameras linked to central monitors all required a considerable amount of space and a great deal of coordination. The main entrance, which was too small for the building's new vocation, was changed and then enhanced by the typical glass-covered steel marquee associated with casinos. Aggregate on lightweight concrete panels helped harmonize the outside walls with those of the Manoir, whose unsurfaced concrete had grown even rougher with time.

*Original casino.*
*Photo: Loto-Québec coll.*

The Casino's glass elevator
Photo: Loto-Québec coll.

During the second phase of the project, three new gaming rooms were built as well as a private lounge with a spectacular view of the St. Lawrence River. From the centre room, a fourth room below could be reached via a monumental staircase and glass elevator. This room also features a wonderful view of the river, which is especially impressive in this location because of its size and the intensive shipping traffic.

The generous use of natural unpainted wood on the walls and ceilings was designed to recreate the hushed atmosphere typical of casinos in the olden days. Lighting fixtures that were designed and made especially by Québec artisans for the Charlevoix Casino help create a warm atmosphere. Some of the cameras, which are omnipresent and indispensable in this kind of establishment, are even incorporated into the lighting in the large rooms.

As we had hoped, the remodeled building fulfills its new role suitably while integrating itself discreetly into the "sensitive" and highly visible environment of the Manoir Richelieu in its Charlevoix setting.

Inside the casino, an impressive quantity of electromechanical items and surveillance cameras, which needed to be accessible at all times, were incorporated into the original high ceiling of the big room. The gallery was renovated and expanded and a spiral staircase leading up to it was installed in a different place than the original stairs in order to make it the central element in the composition.

The new Manoir Richelieu, including its outlying buildings, was enhanced by a land-scape design that incorporated the old gardens and skillfully highlighted the absolute-ly marvelous natural site.

*Ultra-modern interiors of Charlevoix Casino. Photo: Loto-Québec coll.*

# Centennial Celebration

Photos: MR

*Regional Vice-President Philippe Borel
with the Manoir Richelieu's General Manager
Alex Kassatly. Photo: MR*

# CONCLUSION

## REBIRTH OF A LEGEND

*An impressive château perched on its cliff.*
*Photo: MR*

The Manoir Richelieu: a century of resort architecture standing proudly atop a cliff which has left its mark on the whole region; a century of traditions which have been carried on over the years and which have made the prestigious hotel famous.

The Manoir, a Norman château overlooking the mighty St. Lawrence, is remarkable first and foremost for its architecture. The severity of the concrete hotel complex is alleviated by attractive towers and turrets and by the multiple windows and dormers in the steeply pitched copper roofs. Because the additions were all integrated so beautifully, the hotel still creates a perfectly harmonious picture today, characterized by elegance and simplicity.

*The magic
of nightfall.
Photo: MR*

But it is the lavish interiors, so meticulously restored for the year 2000, which overwhelm the hotel's guests and visitors. Originally created by Hugh Coverdale and restored during the latest renovation, the décor is reminiscent of both France and Charlevoix. Staying at the Manoir Richelieu is like being allowed the privilege to go back in time and enjoy a level of luxury worthy of the *belle époque* in the comfort of the twenty-first century.

Welcome to Murray Bay! Nothing is more picturesque, more refreshing, more varied, more gracious than that little corner of the Garden of Eden on the slopes of the Laurentians!

These few lines that so aptly described La Malbaie a hundred years ago are still true today.

# BIBLIOGRAPHY

Canadian Pacific Archives

Canada Steamship Lines Archives

Bulletin des recherches historiques

M.R.L.C. Murray Bay Collection

McGill University, Canadian Architecture Collection and Maxwell Archives, Blackader Lautermann Library

Archives nationales du Québec, Québec

Public Archives of Canada, Ottawa

Archibald, John S., "The New Manoir Richelieu," *Journal of the Royal Architectural Institute of Canada*, September, 1930

Bergeron, Claude, *Architecture du XX siècle*, Québec

Bouchette, Joseph, *A Topographical Dictionary of the Provinces of Lower Canada*, London, 1815

Catalogue, *Manoir Richelieu Collection of Canadiana, Murray Bay, Quebec. Pictural History of the "Siege of Quebec" 1759*, Montréal, Canada Steamship Lines ltd

Coverdale, William Hugh, *Tadoussac, Then and Now*, Printed in Canada, 1942

Des Gagniers, *Charlevoix: Pays enchanté*, Québec, Les Presses de l'Université Laval: 1994

Dubé, Philippe, *Charlevoix: Two Centuries at Murray Bay*, Kingson & Montréal, McGill-Queens University Press: 1990

Fraser, Alex, *Fraser Clan in Canada*, Toronto, Mailjob Printing Co: 1894

Gagnon Pratte, France, *L'architecture et la nature à Québec au XIXe siècle : les villas*, Québec, Ministère des Affaires culturelles and Musée du Québec: 1980

Gagnon Pratte, France, *Country Houses for Montrealers, 1892-1924: The Architecture of E. and W.S. Maxwell*, Montréal, Meridian Press: 1989

Gagnon Pratte, France, *The Banff Springs Hotel*, Québec, Éditions Continuité: 1997

Gagnon Pratte, France, *The Château Frontenac*, Québec, Éditions Continuité: 1993

Garceau, H.P., *Chronique de l'hospitalité hôtelière du Québec, 1880-1940*, Montréal, Éditions du Méridien: 1990

Gingras, Sylvain, *Chasse et pêche au Québec*, Les Éditions Rapides Blancs Inc: 1994

Glickman, M., *The Construction of the Manoir Richelieu*, Technical Paper, Montréal, McGill University, 1961

Hale, Katherine, *Legends of the St. Lawrence*, Montréal, CPR

Kalman, Harold, *A History of Canadian Architecture, Vol. 2*, Toronto, Oxford University Press: 1994

Kalman, Harold, *The Railway Hotels and the Development of the Château Style in Canada*, Victoria, Morris Printing Co: 1968

LeMoine, James McPherson, *Picturesque Québec*, Québec, Dawson Bros: 1882

LeMoine, James McPherson, *Monographies et esquisses*, Québec, 1882

MacPherson, Charlotte H.G., *Reminiscences of Old Quebec*, Montréal, John Lovell & Son: 1890

Maxwell, W.S., "John S. Archibald 1872-1934" in *Journal of the Royal Architectural Institute of Canada*, March 1934, Vol. II

Roy, Pierre-Georges, "Saint-Étienne de la Malbaie," *Bulletin des recherches historiques*, 1895, vol. 1

Roy, Pierre-Georges, *Vieux manoirs, vieilles maisons*, Québec, 1927

Uzzell, Thomas H., *Golf in the World's Oldest Mountains*, Montréal, The Ronalds Company Limited: 1926

*In the winter of 2000, the Manoir Richelieu in all its splendour.*
*Photo: François Rivard*

## ACKNOWLEDGEMENTS

I could not have written this book without the enthusiastic help of many different people: Michel Crète, CEO of Loto-Québec, who believed in the rebirth of the Manoir Richelieu and, with the consortium composed of Canadian Pacific Hotels, Loto-Québec, and the Fonds de solidarité des travailleurs du Québec, supervised the salvaging operation; Kevin Johnson, who gave me access to the archives of the Canada Steamship Lines, which provided much of the research material and iconographic information I needed; Nancy Williatte Battet of Canadian Pacific Archives, who supplied the iconographic information I was lacking; Gilbert Deschamps, an engineer with Canadian Pacific who was helpful right from the beginning, provided me with invaluable information, and organized several tours of the building sites and the Manoir; and designer Alexandra Champalimaud of Alexandra Champalimaud & Associates, architect Paul Gauthier of Gauthier, Guité, Roy, architects Bernard & Cloutier, and Bruce Allan of Groupe Arcop, who all provided me with plans, sketches and texts relating to the restoration and renovation of the Manoir Richelieu.

My thanks also go to graphic designer Norman Dupuis, to translator Linda Blythe, and to Louise Mercier, manager and editor-in-chief of Continuité Press, for her valued contribution to the Grand Hotels of Canada series. Finally, I would like to say that the book *Charlevoix: Two Centuries at Murray Bay* by historian Philippe Dubé – an exhaustive study of resort life at Murray Bay – was an indispensable source of information.